Voices for Freedom
Abolitionist Heroes

By Henry Elliot

FREDERICK DOUGLASS

From Slavery to Statesman

CRABTREE
Publishing Company
www.crabtreebooks.com

D1126813

Author: Henry Elliot
Publishing plan research and development:
  Sean Charlebois, Reagan Miller
  Crabtree Publishing Company
Editors: Mark Sachner, Lynn Peppas
Proofreader: Ellen Rodger
Editorial director: Kathy Middleton
Photo research: Ruth Owen
Designer: Westgrapix/Tammy West
Production coordinator: Margaret Amy Salter
Prepress technician: Margaret Amy Salter
Production: Kim Richardson
Curriculum adviser: Suzy Gazlay, M.A.
Editorial consultant: James Marten, Ph.D.; Chair, Department
  of History, Marquette University, Milwaukee, Wisconsin

Front cover (inset), back cover, and title page: Photograph of
Frederick Douglass.
Front cover (bottom): A series of anti-slavery trading cards from
the 1800s, by American artist Henry Louis Stephens. Pictures like
this were used by abolitionists to convince people that slavery
should be stopped.

Written, developed, and produced by Water Buffalo Books

Publisher's note:
All quotations in this book come from original sources and contain
the spelling and grammatical inconsistencies of the original text.
Some of the quotations may also contain terms that are no longer in
use and may be considered inappropriate or offensive. The use of
such terms is for the sake of preserving the historical and literary
accuracy of the sources and should not be seen as encouraging or
endorsing the use of such terms today.

Photographs and reproductions
Alamy: page 5 (left). Corbis: page 4 (bottom); page 12; page 13;
page 17 (bottom); page 19 (top); page 19 (bottom); page 38; page
53. Findfamilyroots.com: page 39; page 56. Frederick Douglass
National Historic Site: page 20; page 21 (all); page 31 (left). Getty
Images: page 5 (right); page 6; page 7; page 26 (bottom); page 58
(bottom). The Granger Collection: page 11; page 14; page 18
(bottom); page 24 (right); page 27; page 29; page 58 (top). The
Liberator Files: page 22. Courtesy of the Library of Congress:
Image 3a18122: page 1; page 4 (top left); Image 05089: page 8;
Image 3a18122: page 9 (top left); Image 00057: page 9 (left);
Image 0206001: page 17 (top); Image 3a18122: page 18 (top left);
Image 3a45884: page 26 (top); Image 3a18122: page 29 (top left);
Image 0001: page 31 (right); Image 0210001: page 32; Image
12783: page 33 (top); Image 3b29775: page 33 (bottom); Image
3a13608: page 36; Image 3a18122: page 40 (top left); Image
07773: page 42; Image 3b50577: page 45; Image 3a46545: page 48;
Image 3a18122: page 49 (top left); Image 0019: page 49 (bottom);
Image 3a50075u: page 50 (top); Image 3c27756: page 50
(bottom); Image 3b39466: page 54. The Massachusetts Historical
Society: page 47 (bottom). North Wind Archives: page 9
(bottom); page 10; page 24 (left); page 41. Public domain: page
31 (top); page 46 (bottom). Shutterstock: page 40; page 46 (top);
page 46 (center). Superstock: page 34. Wikipedia (public
domain): page 3; page 23; page 28; page 37; page 43; page 44;
page 47 (top); page 55; page 57.

Library and Archives Canada Cataloguing in Publication

Elliot, Henry
    Frederick Douglass : from slavery to statesman / Henry Elliot.

(Voices for freedom: abolitionist heros)
Includes index.
ISBN 978-0-7787-4820-5 (bound).--ISBN 978-0-7787-4836-6 (pbk.)

1. Douglass, Frederick, 1818-1895--Juvenile literature.
2. Abolitionists--United States--Biography--Juvenile literature.
3. African American abolitionists--Biography--Juvenile literature.
4. Antislavery movements--United States--History--19th century--
Juvenile literature. I. Title. II. Series: Voices for freedom:
abolitionist heros

E449.D75E45 2009   j973.8092   C2009-904188-X

Library of Congress Cataloging-in-Publication Data

Elliot, Henry.
  Frederick Douglass : from slavery to statesman / Henry Elliot.
      p. cm. -- (Voices for freedom: abolitionist heros)
  Includes index.
  ISBN 978-0-7787-4836-6 (pbk. : alk. paper) -- ISBN 978-0-7787-
4820-5 (reinforced library binding : alk. paper)
  1. Douglass, Frederick, 1818-1895--Juvenile literature. 2. Aboli-
tionists--United States--Biography--Juvenile literature. 3. African
American abolitionists--Biography--Juvenile literature. 4. Anti-
slavery movements--United States--Juvenile literature. I. Title.
  E449.D75E55 2009
  973.8092--dc22
  [B]
                                                2009027271

Crabtree Publishing Company

www.crabtreebooks.com   1-800-387-7650
Copyright © **2010 CRABTREE PUBLISHING COMPANY.** All rights reserved. No part of this publication may be reproduced, stored in
a retrieval system or be transmitted in any form or by any means, electronic, mechanical, photocopying, recording, or otherwise, without
the prior written permission of Crabtree Publishing Company.

**Published
in Canada
Crabtree Publishing**
616 Welland Ave.
St. Catharines, Ontario
L2M 5V6

**Published in
the United States
Crabtree Publishing**
PMB16A
350 Fifth Ave., Suite 3308
New York, NY 10118

**Published in the
United Kingdom
Crabtree Publishing**
Maritime House
Basin Road North, Hove
BN41 1WR

**Published
in Australia
Crabtree Publishing**
386 Mt. Alexander Rd.
Ascot Vale (Melbourne)
VIC 3032

Contents

CHAPTER ONE

Turning Points

It was August 1833. For six months, Frederick Bailey had been whipped almost every day. Frederick, a 16-year-old African-American slave, was considered "rebellious" by his owner, and the beatings were supposed to make him obedient. Instead, they brought him to the point of desperation. When his keeper, Edward Covey, started to beat him one more time, Frederick did something dangerous and almost unheard of. He fought back.

A "Career" Turning Point

It was a bloody brawl. For two hours, inside of a barn, the slave and his

By 1845, just seven years after his daring escape from slavery, Frederick Douglass had become a gifted orator and writer and a powerful anti-slavery leader. This photo of Douglass was taken around 1855.

The Frederick Douglass Monument in Rochester, New York (above). Dedicated by Governor Theodore Roosevelt in 1899, it is the first public statue of a black man in the United States.

In this photo (above right), believed to have been taken just before the abolition of slavery in 1865, a slave is shown standing with his hands tied to a whipping post as a white man prepares to beat him. As a teenage slave, Frederick Douglass was beaten and whipped almost every day for six months.

keeper punched, kicked, choked, scratched, and struck each other with sticks and other objects. Each man was so exhausted he could barely throw another punch. Covey, the white farmer, declared himself the winner. According to an account of the fight by Frederick himself, however, it was Covey who had been beaten. Also according to Frederick, the fight had made Covey the docile one, and he never beat Frederick again.

In his most famous book, *Narrative of the Life of Frederick Douglass, An American Slave, Written by Himself* (1845), that same slave, Frederick, would write,

An artist's rendition shows the first African slaves brought ashore to the colonies in the early 1600s, almost exactly 200 years before Frederick Douglass was born in 1818. By 1860, there would be four million slaves in the United States and its territories.

> *The battle with Mr. Covey was the turning-point in my career as a slave.*

For this young slave who would become Frederick Douglass, it was not the first turning point of his life; nor would it be the last. From his birth in 1818 until his death in 1895, his life would change many times. And he would witness and help make possible many equally dramatic changes for the United States.

Other Fights

In 1833, slavery was a common and legal practice in the United States. It was especially common on the farms and plantations of the southern states. The first African slaves came to the American colonies in 1619. By 1833, the total number of slaves in the United States had grown to nearly three million. Like Frederick, most of them were born into slavery, not captured, kidnapped, and forced into bondage, and they had never known any other way of life. It was not uncommon for slave owners (or in Covey's case, a slave renter) to beat their slaves, sometimes brutally. It was rare, though, for a slave to stand up and fight back.

Before and after Frederick's brawl with Covey, other fights about slavery were waged in the United States. Some of them were as bloody as Frederick's. Others were worse, with people dying on both sides. Others were fought in the pages of newspapers and in the political arena.

On the one side were pro-slavery forces, on the other were abolitionists, people dedicated to bringing slavery to an end. Pro-slavery people were not just slave owners, and they were not only Americans who lived in the slave states of the South. Many citizens of free states did profitable business with, and supported, slave owners. Others were uncomfortable living among the growing population of free blacks. Until the 1850s, most northerners just didn't feel strongly enough either way to take sides.

Punching and Counterpunching

Abolitionist and pro-slavery Americans battled back and forth, sometimes politically, sometimes violently. New York made slavery illegal in 1827, but that same year Georgia made it illegal to educate slaves. Throughout the 1830s and 1840s, pro-slavery riots rocked many free-state cities. In 1831, not quite two years before Frederick's brawl with Covey, an African-American preacher and slave, Nat Turner, led a violent slave rebellion in Virginia. Fifty-seven white people were killed. Eventually, Turner was captured, tried, hanged, and gruesomely skinned. In the months that followed,

In 1831, a slave named Nat Turner led a violent slave revolt in Virginia, just 160 miles (260 kilometers) from Frederick Douglass' slave home. The rebellion left 57 white people dead. Within days, more than 100 African Americans were killed in retaliation.

individual slave owners, slave patrols, militia units, and local courts pursued and executed slaves who were thought to be involved in the uprising. In the process, many innocent slaves were also killed.

As Frederick's life continued to change, so would the political landscape of America. When he escaped from slavery in 1838, abolitionists were organizing the Underground Railroad, a secret network of sympathizers who provided safe havens for thousands of runaway slaves. When Frederick became an abolitionist leader, he strengthened the numbers and the clout of the abolitionist movement. When he consulted with President Abraham Lincoln, Frederick helped shape the agenda of the Civil War. When he wrote editorials and gave rousing speeches, he influenced Congress to free all slaves and grant black men the right to vote.

After the Civil War, Frederick broke new ground for people of color. He was nominated as a candidate for vice president of the United States, ran a bank, and served in several important political appointments. He also wrote two more autobiographies. By the time he died in 1895, these and other achievements had made Frederick Douglass one of the most important figures in American history.

After the Civil War and the abolition of slavery, Frederick Douglass continued to break new ground for black Americans in the fields of politics, business, publishing, and literature. He became respected and known to all Americans as "The Lion of Anacostia"—a reference to the affluent neighborhood in Washington, D.C., where Douglass later lived.

CHAPTER TWO

Slavery and Escape

Like many slaves, Frederick did not know the exact day and year when he was born. No birth certificate exists recording the date, time, or location of his birth. It is usually accepted that he was born in 1818. Because he remembered his mother calling him her "little valentine," he preferred to think he was a Valentine's Day child, born on February 14. Whatever his exact birthday, in the eyes of the world at large, the baby slave was just one more piece of personal property.

In this photo (left), taken in 1862, five generations of a slave family are shown on a plantation in South Carolina. In the illustration on the right, an African-American slave is shown taking care of her children. In addition to physical brutalities, slaves also lived in fear of being torn away from beloved family members and never seeing them again. Slaves were "property," so an owner could sell a husband to one farm and a child to another and keep the mother for himself. As a child, Frederick barely knew his mother, who was "rented" to a farm 12 miles (19 km) away.

An Uncertain Ancestry

His birth name was Frederick Augustus Washington Bailey, and Frederick did not rename himself until many years later. His mother was Harriet Bailey, but Frederick was raised mostly by his grandmother, Betsey. It is thought that Betsey was part Native American. Harriet worked long days in fields 12 miles (19 km) away and then had to walk back to the plantation where she lived. The identity of Frederick's father is not known for certain, but it's a good guess he was Harriet's part owner and overseer, Aaron Anthony. If so, Frederick was a slave with African, Native American, and European blood.

The Big House

Most children born into slavery were introduced into the work routine of a farm or plantation. Most slave children generally started doing chores and taking care of even younger children. They would not become "full hands" until they were about 12 years old. Frederick's experiences were somewhat unusual in that his first jobs were in the big house, where his masters lived. Within the cruel world of slavery, his early life as a slave was relatively gentle.

About the time he turned seven, Frederick was assigned to service in the plantation house. Mostly he performed chores for Aaron Anthony's daughter, Lucretia. If Anthony was indeed Frederick's father, then Frederick was serving his own half-sister!

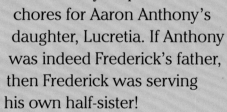

This illustration shows men being served drinks by a young slave in a Louisiana plantation home. Most slaves worked in farm fields under the harshest of conditions. For a while, as a child, Frederick was spared this fate when he worked as a slave servant in his master's house.

As a slave, Frederick could be traded, rented, sold, or loaned. Shortly after his plantation house assignment, he was loaned to Lucretia's husband, Thomas Auld. Thomas then passed Frederick on to his brother, Hugh. Frederick's new masters were Hugh and Sophia Auld, and they lived in the seaport neighborhood of Fells Point in Baltimore. He did not know it at the time, but this move would prove to be a major turning point in Frederick's life. Later, he called it "an act of Providence" (the protective care of God), the first of many that Frederick believed had touched his life.

You Can't Teach Slaves!

Frederick felt he was treated well in the Auld house. He was trusted and often sent on errands out into the exciting neighborhood. Baltimore bustled, and many free blacks crisscrossed the thoroughfare. His mistress, Sophia, not only trusted young Frederick but treated him with kindness and respect. Even more, she taught Frederick some basics of reading and writing.

From the 1892 edition of his autobiography, young Frederick is seen "learning his letters" from his mistress, Sophia Auld. Sophia's husband, Hugh, put a quick end to these lessons.

At the time in Maryland and in all other states in which slavery was legal, teaching slaves was a crime. Sophia was in no danger of being arrested, but her husband, Hugh, laid down the law. Hugh believed it was dangerous to teach a slave to read. He scolded Sophia, "If you teach this nigger to read, there would be no keeping him. It would forever unfit him to be a slave. He would at once become unmanageable, and of no value to his master."

With the help of a piece of chalk, fences to write on, and some of the white children in the neighborhood, Frederick kept up with his lessons. As he continued to read and interact with the people of Baltimore, he learned that some people believed slavery

When Frederick was assigned as a "field hand" in 1833, work conditions were much like those depicted in this engraving. Backbreaking manual labor for men, women, and children was typical.

was wrong and that slaves were known to escape to the North, where they could be free. The idea of freedom began to rattle in his brain and heart.

Setbacks

By his early teens, Frederick had something most slaves had all too little of—hope. All that quickly changed. Though Hugh and Sophia were his masters, they did not own him. In 1833, his owner, Aaron Anthony, died. Anthony's "property," including Frederick, had to be divided up among his heirs. Thomas Auld inherited Frederick, and Frederick found himself scooped away from Baltimore and back on the plantation.

For the first time, Frederick was subjected to backbreaking work in the fields. Just as Hugh Auld had warned his wife, as a slave Frederick was ruined. He objected to work conditions, and he incited other slaves to do the same. The owners of the surrounding farms allowed their slaves to attend unsupervised Bible study on Sundays. Frederick used this chance to teach his fellow slaves to read. His "class" had grown to 40 students before the slaves' masters caught on and stopped these lessons. To his own master, Thomas, Frederick was trouble waiting to happen.

That's when Thomas sent Frederick to the "slave breaker," Edward Covey. If you had a rebellious slave, Covey was your man. For six months, Covey whipped Frederick almost daily. Looking back on this time, Frederick admitted that the slave breaker had won. Frederick stopped reading. He lost his intellectual curiosity. He questioned his belief in God, and he even contemplated suicide:

> *I was broken in body, soul, and spirit ... the dark night of slavery closed in upon me.*

A Glorious Resurrection

Then came Frederick's fight with Covey, an event that would once again set Frederick's life off in a new direction. Later in his life, Douglass called the fight "a glorious resurrection, from the tomb of slavery, to the heaven of freedom" —but it almost didn't happen.

After a particularly brutal beating that left him bloody, Frederick staggered 7 miles (11 km) to Thomas Auld's house to plead for help. His master just sent him back to Covey. It was then that Frederick had the two-hour brawl with Covey that would end the beatings for good. Covey could have told Thomas Auld about Frederick's one-man rebellion. He could have demanded "justice." He could have argued for Frederick to be whipped and starved,

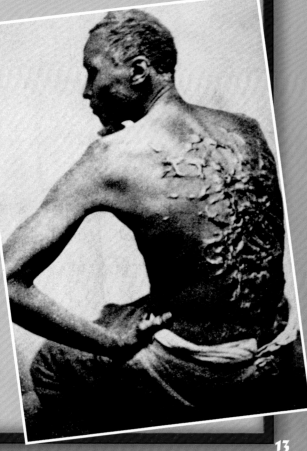

During his time under the supervision of "slave breaker" Edward Covey, Frederick was whipped or beaten almost daily. In this photo, a former slave shows the scars of his brutal whippings.

or even that he should be killed as a warning to other slaves, but none of these happened. Our knowledge of this event comes only from Frederick's autobiography, so we don't know for sure exactly what went on in Covey's head after the fight. It may have been that Covey was ashamed that he was beaten by a 16-year-old slave, but whatever the reason, Covey never told a soul.

Two Unsuccessful Tries

Even before his brutal time with Covey the slave breaker, Frederick had vowed to escape. He made a clumsy effort in 1833, and it failed. His attempt was one of the reasons he was sent to Covey in the first place. Even though Covey never again beat Frederick after their fight, Frederick despised his bondage more than ever. When Thomas Auld "transferred" Frederick from Covey to another farmer, a man named Mr. Freeman, in 1836, Frederick hatched a second plan. This one was better and more sophisticated, but the end result was the same.

This illustration from the 1892 edition of Frederick's autobiography shows him hiding in the woods after running away from Covey's farm. In Frederick's account, he meets a fellow slave named Sandy (shown here), who gives Frederick a "magic root" to protect him from harm and tells him to return to Covey. Following Frederick's return, he and Covey got into the fight in which Frederick beat up Covey.

On Freeman's farm, Frederick forged passes for a few fellow slaves and himself. These passes claimed that their master permitted them to go to Baltimore for the Easter holidays. Their real plan was to reach Baltimore, then escape to Pennsylvania by boat.

Before they could put their plan into action, one of Frederick's co-conspirators backed out. He betrayed Frederick and the others. Several of Mr. Freeman's white employees grabbed Frederick. While being dragged from his slave quarters, Frederick managed without notice to throw his forged pass into the fireplace. He denied everything about any escape plans. Without "hard" evidence, Frederick received an unusually mild punishment of a week in jail.

After his week in jail, Frederick caught another lucky break when he once again was sent to Baltimore to work for Hugh Auld. There, in 1838, he formulated a third escape plan. This time his plan would be better. This time he would have help. This time it would work.

Aided by Geography

Any attempt at escape was considered daring and dangerous. But for those willing to take the chance, Baltimore was a good place to try. Here, slaves were not confined to a farm, and they often walked the city streets without supervision.

In addition to the increased chances for escape that this situation provided, Maryland bordered the free state of Pennsylvania. This meant a shorter distance to travel to get to the North than from the Carolinas or Georgia.

Allies

Back with the Aulds in Baltimore, Frederick was hired out to work in the shipyards as a caulker. Although Frederick provided the labor, it was Auld who received the paycheck, usually about six dollars a week ($120 today). The work was hard, and often he was abused by the white workers. Once he was beaten senseless and bloody. No one helped him. Still, there were advantages to his new situation. Frederick was treated kindly by the Aulds.

He was permitted to attend church and to mingle with Baltimore's free blacks. In those respects, his life as a slave had never been better, but the more that life improved, the stronger his desire grew to be free. Frederick's freedom was at hand.

It was through church that he met Anna Murray, a free black woman, and it was in the shipyards that he met a sympathetic merchant sailor. Both Anna and the sailor, who was also a free black, helped Frederick plan his escape.

A Penny Saved

Frederick resented the fact that he had to turn all of his wages over to his master. To ease his conscience, for a while Hugh Auld sometimes gave Frederick a few pennies. Hugh and Frederick later made a deal. Hugh let Frederick find his own work and keep his own wages. In return, Frederick had to give his master three dollars a week plus two dollars and 50 cents for room and board. He also had to rent or buy his own caulking tools.

This meant that Frederick had to earn more than six dollars a week to have anything left for himself. Auld eventually decided to end this agreement, but not before Frederick was able to put away a few dollars.

With his small savings and some more money from his friend Anna, Frederick now hatched his escape plan. At the time, free blacks had to carry identification papers that showed they were not slaves. This was before photo IDs, so the papers had only the person's name, age, height, weight, and general description. If a slave closely matched the description of a free black, he or she could buy or borrow those papers and leave Maryland in the guise of a free black.

Frederick and his friend the black merchant sailor were close to the same size. Using the money he had saved, Frederick was able to buy this man's papers and clothing, which would have identified him as a merchant seaman. Using money Anna gave him, Frederick bought a railroad ticket and boarded a train from Baltimore to Philadelphia.

Success!

Frederick was terrified that he would be discovered at any moment. His heart raced as fast as the train. His papers were checked. No questions were asked. He could scarcely believe it. Within hours, Frederick found himself in the free city of Philadelphia. The next day, he was in New York City, where his life as a slave finally seemed to be at an end—and his life as a fugitive would begin.

During slavery, free blacks without identification might find themselves imprisoned as runaway slaves. To prevent that from happening, they carried official documents certifying they were free citizens. Frederick Douglass used a sympathetic African-American seaman's papers, which were similar to these, to pose as a free black and escape from slavery.

At about the time Frederick Douglass used a train to escape from slavery in Baltimore, railroads were still something of a novelty. Here, in a publicity stunt, an early steam locomotive races against a horse-drawn carriage.

CHAPTER THREE

The Invention of Frederick Douglass

At the time of his escape, Frederick Bailey was 20 years old. Almost immediately, he began to make changes to his life. Out of necessity, he changed his last name. Within the span of one week, Frederick's last name went from Bailey to Stanley to Johnson to Douglass. As a fugitive from slavery, he had a price on his head for his capture and return. Changing his name helped him stay one step ahead of the bounty hunters. This was just the first of many steps Frederick took over the next seven years to reinvent himself as a free man. Of course, once he settled on Douglass, he stuck with it, and that is the name we know him by today.

Frederick's early years in New Bedford were a time of rapid growth for him, and he soon became a prominent citizen. This oil painting, done in the 1840s, is one of the earliest known portraits of the young Frederick Douglass.

Above: At the time of Frederick's escape, the river ports and seaports of New York City offered easy travel for passengers to other towns along the East Coast.

Left: Frederick was greeted with the hustle and bustle of scenes such as this when he arrived in New York City just days after his escape from slavery.

A Jumble of Feelings

When he reached New York, Frederick said it was "the highest excitement I ever experienced." Seeing a house with a pile of coal in front, he knocked on the door and offered to shovel the coal into the chute. It was hard work, but when he was done, he had earned a dollar. It was his to keep. As he realized that he had escaped the economics of slavery, a thrill raced through his entire being. Within the next few days, however, his emotions would bounce from joy to fear to despair and back again.

Trust No Man

Frederick's initial excitement was soon replaced by fear and loneliness. His escape was a deep secret that he could not share with anyone. He walked the streets afraid of being kidnapped and returned to slavery. His motto was "trust no man," white or black.

Money was another problem. He was flat broke. He needed to find an odd job or two each day just to eat and get a place to sleep for the night.

Things were happening fast. At the time Frederick escaped, he had heard of a network of abolitionists in New York and New England. They gave Frederick lodging and a few dollars. One helped him get to New Bedford, Massachusetts. Another helped Frederick bring Anna Murray, the free black woman he had met in Baltimore, to New Bedford, where they were married the next day. All of this happened within the first week after Frederick had escaped.

Anna Murray, a free black woman, was very fond of Frederick. She gave him some money to help finance his escape. She would also become his wife.

Job Applications

Now it was time to find work, and Frederick roamed the streets looking for employment. He came to New Bedford because it was a seaport town. He had experience as a caulker and thought he would find work on the docks, but all the caulking jobs were held by prejudiced white men. They would not work with African Americans, so there was no work there.

Despite this bitter reality, New Bedford surprised Frederick with "splendid churches, beautiful dwellings, and finely cultivated gardens." More so, he was astonished to see African Americans, many of them escaped slaves, living in middle-class comfort.

After three days in New Bedford, Frederick found work as a handyman doing odd jobs. When he collected his first wages, he called the moment "the starting point of a new existence," another turning point in his life. For three years, he did not lack for work.

Love and Marriage

Frederick and Anna remained married until her death in 1882. Although they were not always close, they had five children: Rosetta (1839), Lewis (1840), Frederick, Jr. (1842), Charles (1844), and Annie (1849). Lewis and Frederick Jr. would serve as soldiers in an all-black regiment in the Civil War. Rosetta and Charles would work with their father in publishing. Annie died when she was ten.

Frederick hired several tutors, but Anna never learned to read or write. This was a great disappointment to Frederick, and it strained their relationship. Although they never divorced, Frederick had several romances with other women during their marriage.

Portraits of the Douglass children. From top to bottom: Charles, Frederick Jr., Rosetta, and Lewis. Another daughter, Annie, died at the age of ten.

Frederick the Abolitionist

In January 1839, four months after Frederick's arrival in New Bedford, a weekly newspaper, *The Liberator*, fell into Frederick's hands. He read every word of it. *The Liberator* was published by the famous abolitionist William Lloyd Garrison. Like its publisher, *The Liberator* was dedicated to the immediate end of all slavery in the United States. Frederick thought that abolitionists were a loose group of kind and well-intentioned people, but he had not been particularly impressed with their being militant or highly organized. Reading *The Liberator* changed that impression. It taught him that abolitionists used language and organization as weapons to attack slavery. It brought him to the brink of yet another change. He wrote,

> *It sent a thrill of joy through my soul such as I had never felt before.*

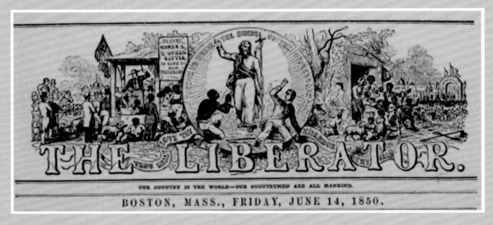

BOSTON, MASS., FRIDAY, JUNE 14, 1850.

The "masthead" of William Lloyd Garrison's abolitionist newspaper, *The Liberator*. The scenes on the masthead show a slave auction (left), a slave praying to Jesus (center) as his master is driven off, and the glorious emancipation of the slaves.

One thing led to another. Soon Frederick was attending anti-slavery meetings. When he heard Garrison speak in 1841, Garrison became his hero. The eloquence and power of his words convinced Frederick that public speaking, when done well, could change opinions, politics, and the world. A few days later, he gave his first speech before a mostly white audience of the Massachusetts Anti-Slavery Society. He was shaking and nervous. He heard his voice crack. He did not think he had done a very good job. Society leaders thought differently. Almost immediately, he was hired by the Society as a professional lecturer.

William Lloyd Garrison

William Lloyd Garrison (1805–1879) is generally regarded as the leader of the abolitionist movement. He is best known as the publisher of *The Liberator*, an abolitionist newspaper, and as the founder of the American Anti-Slavery Society (AAS). *The Liberator* was published from 1831 until 1866. It never had a circulation of more than 3,000, but it was banned in several southern states. Garrison was also a strong supporter of women's rights. In 1840, when he opened the AAS to female membership, many male members disagreed and quit the organization.

Although Garrison was a pacifist, he made one exception where he felt violence was needed to further the cause of the complete abolition of slavery in all of the United States. That exception was the Civil War, and Garrison was a firm supporter of the Union cause.

A statue of William Lloyd Garrison by Olin Levi Warner (1844–1896), located on Commonwealth Avenue in Boston.

Douglass the Orator

During the next four years, Frederick Douglass, the escaped slave and day laborer, became Frederick Douglass, the orator. Before he even spoke, Douglass could impress an audience with his "podium presence." He was tall and robust. He wore stylish and dignified suits. His eyes were said to be fiery.

Then he would speak. His voice was strong and deep. He knew when to pause, and he knew when to raise his voice. He knew how to make his listeners laugh and how to make

From the very start, Douglass had charisma and a commanding presence that held the attention of his audience. As he became more experienced, his oratorical skills were often compared with those of Abraham Lincoln.

them squirm. He used effective speaking techniques to hammer his message home.

Here is an example from a speech he gave in 1841, when he had very little experience as a speaker. The speech is about the hypocrisy of members of a church that preaches against slavery and prejudice. The members go to church every Sunday, but they do not follow its teachings:

> Yet people in general will say they like colored men as well as any other, but in their proper place! They assign us that place; they don't let us do it for ourselves, nor will they allow us a voice in the decision.

They will not allow that we have a head to think,
and a heart to feel, and a soul to aspire.
They treat us not as men, but as dogs—they cry
"Stu-boy!" and expect us to run and do their bidding.
That's the way we are liked. You degrade us,
and then ask why we are degraded—you shut
our mouths, and then ask why we don't
speak—you close our colleges and seminaries
against us, and then ask why we don't know more.

The Six-Month Marathon

During the course of six months in 1843, Frederick attended and spoke at 100 conventions. Conventions were major events held once a year or so; these appearances probably included regular meetings and special lectures of Anti-Slavery and Women's Rights groups. His concerns were not just slavery in the South. He also attacked racial prejudice in the North. The more he spoke, the more his reputation grew. The more his reputation grew, the more closely he and Garrison worked together. His effectiveness as a speaker also caused controversy. Many people refused to believe his stories. They claimed it was impossible for a former slave to speak so powerfully. They claimed Frederick Douglass was an impostor. Frederick felt the need to prove his doubters wrong.

Frederick Douglass the Activist and Fighter

Frederick's speeches were acts of activism against slavery and fights for social justice. He also did more. In an act that foreshadowed Rosa Parks and the Montgomery bus boycott of 1955, Douglass refused to move from a "white only" passenger car on a train in New England, in 1841. Train conductors forcibly removed him from the car. News of this led to a boycott of the railroad by abolitionists. More and more African Americans boarded the trains and refused to sit in the car reserved for black passengers. After months of conflict, the railroad relented and allowed integrated cars.

In 1843, Douglass was speaking in Indiana when a pro-slavery mob attacked him and his audience. Although he tried to abide by Garrison's code of nonviolent resistance, Frederick was seized by the same impulse that had brought him to blows with Covey. When he saw people in his audience being punched, he leapt from the podium, picked up a branch, and fought back. Although injured, Douglass held his own. Others in the crowd were not so lucky, and many were hurt.

Left: This newspaper illustration shows a scene similar to what Douglass experienced in 1841, when he sat in a "whites only" railway car and was forcibly removed.

Below: More than 100 years later, in 1955, the black citizens of Montgomery, Alabama, organized a bus boycott when Rosa Parks sat among white passengers and refused to move to the back of the bus. This photograph shows Parks (center) and other passengers riding on a newly integrated Montgomery bus following the successful completion of the boycott.

Putting Pen to Paper

Although Frederick became established as an important abolitionist, by 1845 he felt he was in a rut. He needed to add power to his personal and public life. First, he needed money. The lecture circuit was more than a full-time job for Frederick, but it didn't pay very well. Anna took in sewing and laundry to help, but the Douglasses had children to raise, and they lived without some of the comforts they desired. Second, Frederick was still nagged by people who continued to doubt his credentials. Third, he wanted more clout—more power and an even stronger voice—in his fight for abolition.

He envisioned a solution to all three challenges. It was a book.

Narrative of the Life of Frederick Douglass

In 1845, Frederick Douglass wrote and published *Narrative of the Life of Frederick Douglass, An American Slave, Written By Himself*. Today, this book is studied in almost every class unit on 19th century American literature. Compared to Harriet Beecher Stowe's *Uncle Tom's Cabin* (1852), an anti-slavery novel, sales of Frederick's autobiography were very modest. Stowe's novel sold 300,000 copies in its first year.

In a rare incidence of violence, Frederick used a club to fight off attackers who tried to break up his 1843 outdoor speech in Indiana. This illustration is from the 1892 edition of his autobiography.

NARRATIVE

OF THE

LIFE

OF

FREDERICK DOUGLASS,

AN

AMERICAN SLAVE.

WRITTEN BY HIMSELF.

BOSTON:

PUBLISHED AT THE ANTI-SLAVERY OFFICE,

No. 25 CORNHILL

1845.

The title page of Douglass' 1845 *Narrative*, the best known of his three autobiographies. It would go on to sell 11,000 copies in his lifetime.

Between 1845 and 1850, 11,000 people bought Frederick's book. Still, by mid-1800s standards, the book was a commercial success. Soon after its first appearance, it was translated and published in French and Dutch. It doubled Douglass' income and increased the fees he could command for speaking. He was more in demand than ever, and his popularity soared.

Frederick's book swayed many northerners to join the abolitionist cause and moved many part-time abolitionists to a full-time commitment. So he increased his income, and he had more clout. Frederick still had his detractors, however. The writing was so good that many doubters were more convinced than ever that no former slave could write that well.

CHAPTER FOUR

The Reinvention of Frederick Douglass

First published in 1845, the *Narrative of the Life of Frederick Douglass* recalls Frederick's life from his earliest recollections through his escape from Baltimore. More than a million copies have sold since Frederick's death. Frederick would go on to write two more autobiographies. *My Bondage and My Freedom* (1855) continues his story from his escape through his career as an abolitionist. In 1881, he published the third of his autobiographical volumes. In *Life and Times of Frederick Douglass*, Frederick writes of his life through and after the Civil War.

With each successive autobiography, Douglass expanded upon his life as a slave. This illustration from *My Bondage and My Freedom* (1855) accompanies Frederick's telling of a sadistic overseer, Mr. Gore, who shot and killed the slave George Denby. Gore went unpunished. This story did not appear in Douglass' *Narrative* of 1845.

Written by "Himself"?

The *Narrative* is an example of writing known as a "slave narrative." It is the most famous of its kind.

Today, most teachers and readers consider the *Narrative* the best written of all slave narratives. It is so skillful that Frederick's doubters could not accept that he could write a memoir with such vivid detail, artful use of metaphor, and polished technique. The same mastery of language that made Douglass such a powerful speaker may be seen on almost every page of the *Narrative*. For example, here is how he writes of his grandmother's death:

> *She stands—she sits—she staggers—she falls—she groans— she dies—and there are none of her children or grandchildren present, to wipe from her wrinkled brow the cold sweat of death....*

Giving Up His Identity

In writing his 1845 *Narrative*, Douglass was intentionally sketchy about how he escaped from Baltimore. In particular, he left out the names of people who helped him, including the role played by his wife-to-be, Anna. The reason was that anyone who helped a slave escape could be arrested and prosecuted. As early as 1793, there were laws, known as Fugitive Slave Laws, that made it a crime to help a slave escape. Frederick wanted to protect their identities. In fact, writing and publishing the *Narrative* blew his own cover. Many abolitionists already knew parts of Frederick's story. The *Narrative*, however, broadcast the news that Frederick Bailey, the runaway slave, was one and the same as Frederick Douglass, the abolitionist lecturer. Despite living in freedom for seven years, Frederick was still a fugitive slave. For a handsome reward, a determined bounty hunter could capture Douglass, use his book to prove he was a runaway, and then bring him back to Baltimore.

Slave Narratives

A slave narrative is a special kind of autobiography about the writer's life as a slave. Examples go as far back as 1760, and they continued to be written through the 1930s.

Three well-known examples include *Life of William Grimes, the Runaway Slave* (1825), *A Narrative of Adventure and Escape of Moses Roper from American Slavery* (1837), and *Incidents in the Life of a Slave Girl* (1861), by Harriet Jacobs.

Harriet Jacobs, author of an early slave narrative, *Incidents in the Life of a Slave Girl*. Jacobs' book is especially revealing in its details about the sexual abuse of young female slaves.

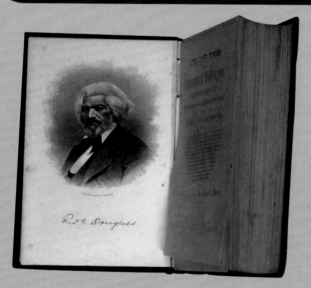

The book and a manuscript page of Douglass' third autobiography, *Life and Times of Frederick Douglass* (1881, revised and expanded 1892). This is the most complete and detailed story of his life.

To dodge this risk, Frederick said goodbye to Anna and his children and fled the United States. He spent the next 21 months giving lectures throughout Ireland and Great Britain. Although his motive was his personal safety, this trip proved to be another major turning point. It brought him international celebrity and his official freedom.

$706.11

Douglass arrived in Ireland about the same time as the Great Potato Famine. Poverty was widespread. Yet he sensed something there that he did not feel in the United States. He said that he was "treated not as a color but as a man."

At the time, it was possible to buy a slave's freedom by paying his owner an agreed-upon price. Frederick's supporters in England collected the 150 British pounds needed to purchase him, the equal of $706.11 (about $14,000 today), and set him free. Frederick was no longer a runaway slave. He was a free black man.

An undated front page of the *North Star*, the abolitionist newspaper Douglass founded and published when he moved to Rochester, New York, in 1847. In 1851, he merged the *North Star* with Gerrit Smith's *Liberal Party Paper*. They named their new publication *Frederick Douglass' Paper.*

Life in Rochester

Returning to the United States in 1847, Frederick moved Anna and their children to Rochester, New York. Rochester was an exciting but divided city, and Frederick helped make it so. There, in the basement of an all-black church, he founded a newspaper, the *North Star*. Frederick served as reporter, editor, and publisher. By now, he had become the equal to, and not the disciple of, his old hero and mentor, William Lloyd Garrison. Garrison did not like this new development. He objected to Frederick's move to Rochester, and he saw the *North Star* as competition to his paper, *The Liberator*.

Soon other abolitionists, white and black, also moved to Rochester to join forces with Douglass and work with him on the paper. Some Rochester citizens were unhappy about their city being home to an abolitionist newspaper, and some even plotted to sabotage his printing presses. Others cheered his efforts and those of another Rochester citizen, Susan B. Anthony, and her women's rights movement.

A Question of Responsibility

The Rochester years were a time of rapid political and intellectual growth for Frederick. With Anna's help, he soon opened his home and newspaper offices as stops on the Underground Railroad where runaway slaves could find safety, shelter, and help.

Susan B. Anthony (1820–1906) in an undated photo (above) and a photographic portrait from the late 1880s (right). In the late 1840s, Anthony was Douglass' fellow activist in Rochester. Together, they helped make Rochester a hotbed of political reform. Anthony is best known as a fighter for women's rights, especially the right to vote. It was in Rochester in 1872 that she organized a group of 50 women who demanded that they be registered to vote. Anthony actually cast her ballot, and a few weeks later she was arrested for this "crime." In 1920, 14 years after she died, the United States ratified the 19th Amendment to the Constitution. A woman's right to vote was finally the law of the land.

At the same time, Douglass was harshly critical of many fellow members of the Underground Railroad. He disapproved of their speaking publicly and writing about their involvement and methods. Frederick saw this as irresponsible. It "taught" slave owners and slave hunters how the Railroad worked and put many runaways at risk.

The *North Star* was a groundbreaking achievement in publishing. It was a newspaper published by a former slave! Unfortunately, it did not make money, and soon Frederick was back on the lecture circuit. Even after six months of giving speeches, he was forced to take out a loan. It wasn't until 1851 that the *North Star* started to make money and support the Douglass family. Taking advantage of his status as a political celebrity, Frederick soon changed the paper's name to *Frederick Douglass' Paper*. He continued to publish the paper until the end of the Civil War.

This 1893 painting by American artist Charles Webber shows runaway slaves receiving help from members of the Underground Railroad. As early as the late 1840s, Frederick Douglass opened his home and the offices of his newspaper as places where escaping slaves could receive food, shelter, and help in making it to the next Underground Railroad "station."

Progressive, but Only Up to a Point

Rochester was a progressive city, and despite the relative few who resented the presence of a prominent abolitionist newspaper, most of its citizens readily accepted the sight of black men and white men in conversation or sitting at the same table. A black man and a white woman were another matter. While he was in England, Frederick met Julia Griffiths, and when he returned home, Julia came with him. Julia tutored Anna and the Douglass children, lived in the Douglass home, and worked as the *North Star* business manager. She and Frederick became constant companions, and the people of Rochester were shocked to see the couple walking arm and arm in the thoroughfares. On a trip to New York City, Frederick and Julia were victims of a violent attack. At least in Rochester, all they got were dirty looks.

Julia was a co-founder of the Rochester Ladies' Anti-Slavery and Sewing Society. This group of abolitionist women sold crafts, published and sold books, and sponsored lectures. They soon were raising $1,500 per year (about $30,000 today). They used the money to support *Frederick Douglass' Paper* and fugitive slaves. The Society was targeted by pro-slavery groups. The political pressure Julia could take, but the personal attacks on her relationship with Frederick Douglass were too much. In 1855, Julia returned to England.

A Dissident Among Dissidents

In his political views, as well as in his personal life, Frederick became less and less influenced by others and more of an independent thinker. In a stunning development, after ten years of working side by side, Frederick broke ranks with his former mentor, William Lloyd Garrison.

Garrison had always argued that the Constitution was pro-slavery and that the United States government should be dissolved. In an 1851 speech, Douglass declared his beliefs that the Constitution could be the basis for full equal rights for all Americans. He blasted Garrison's position on breaking up the United States. He argued this would strand slaves in southern states and take away their chances of escape. Their disagreement became bitter.

When Harriet Beecher Stowe, the author of *Uncle Tom's Cabin*, tried to bring the two back together, Frederick refused. Further, he strongly disagreed with Stowe on the issue of returning freed slaves to Africa. He told her,

> *The truth is, dear madam, we are here, and here we are likely to remain.*

Later, after the Civil War, Frederick also disputed a cause long championed by the women's movement—the right of women to vote. The women's Equal Rights Association insisted there be no voting rights for black men until there were also voting rights for women. Douglass supported women's suffrage, but he condemned this position as naive and idealistic.

The Fourth of July

Though much of his fame now rested on his achievements as a writer, publisher, and activist, Frederick continued to make speeches. One of his most famous is the "Fourth of July." Actually delivered on the fifth of July in 1852, this was a shocking

Because of the immense popularity of her abolitionist novel, *Uncle Tom's Cabin*, Harriet Beecher Stowe was a celebrity and a close associate with the most influential abolitionists of her day. Frederick Douglass was a frequent guest at her home, even though they disagreed on the issue of "repatriating" freed slaves to Africa.

Ottilie Assing

Soon after Julia Griffiths returned to England, Frederick met another supporter. Ottilie Assing (1819–1884), a Jewish woman from Germany, was wealthy, brilliant, and committed to social change. For 26 years she and Frederick were very close friends. When Anna Douglass died in 1882, Ottilie was sure she and Frederick would marry. Instead, Frederick married his much younger secretary, Helen Pitts. Devastated, Ottilie walked to a park, swallowed cyanide, and fell over dead. Yet even in death she continued to support Frederick by leaving him her entire fortune.

A photograph of Frederick Douglass with his second wife, Helen Pitts, and her sister, Eva. Frederick and Helen were married in 1884. After Frederick's death, Helen helped found the Frederick Douglass Memorial and Historical Association. Their mixed-race marriage shocked their families and many supporters.

and vehement speech. Frederick goaded his audience into seeing Independence Day from a slave's point of view.

To the slave, Douglass proclaimed, "your celebration is a sham; your boasted liberty, an unholy license; … your shouts of liberty and equality, hollow mockery." His words foreshadowed those of black activist Malcolm X 125 years later, when Malcolm cried out, in reference to the landing of early British settlers in Plymouth, Massachusetts: "We didn't land on Plymouth Rock; Plymouth Rock landed on us!" Frederick called the holiday "a thin veil to cover up crimes." Anyone who celebrated the Fourth of July was a hypocrite.

People may have criticized slavery, but they did not pledge their lives and fortunes to fight it. In Douglass' own words:

> *For it is not light that is needed, but fire;*
> *it is not the gentle shower, but thunder.*
> *We need the storm, the whirlwind,*
> *and the earthquake. The feeling of the*
> *nation must be quickened; the conscience*
> *of the nation must be roused;*
> *the propriety of the nation must be startled;*
> *the hypocrisy of the nation must be exposed;*
> *and its crimes against God and man*
> *must be proclaimed and denounced.*

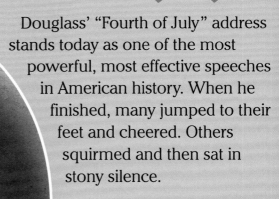

Douglass' "Fourth of July" address stands today as one of the most powerful, most effective speeches in American history. When he finished, many jumped to their feet and cheered. Others squirmed and then sat in stony silence.

The Autobiography Continues

In 1855, at the age of 37, Frederick was filled with boundless energy and creativity.

He published the works of other writers. He edited. He lectured. He helped runaway slaves escape. He also wrote his second autobiography, *My Bondage and My Freedom*.

Much of the book richly expands the story he told ten years earlier in the *Narrative*. In *My Bondage and My Freedom*, he offers a look at the 21 months he spent in Great Britain and Ireland as a fugitive. One of the most valuable features can be found in the appendix, which reprints the full text of many of his most famous speeches up to then.

Douglass' life and accomplishments were already among the most important in American history. By the 1850s, he and the United States of America were about to approach another brink. The winds began to howl.

A photograph of Douglass' desk and study in Cedar Hill, his Washington, D.C., home. Unlike some other abolitionists, Douglass remained as active as ever as a writer and lecturer. It was at this desk where Douglass would write and revise much of his third autobiography, *The Life and Times of Frederick Douglass*.

CHAPTER FIVE

The Storm Builds

Throughout the 1850s, the battle between abolitionist and pro-slavery Americans went from philosophical argument, to angry debate, to merciless violence. It culminated in 1861 with the previously unimaginable loss of life in the great Civil War.

Compromise and Outrage

In 1850, Congress tried to appease both sides with a group of bills known as the Compromise of 1850. Virginia was admitted to the Union as a free state. The slave trade in the District of Columbia was abolished (although

This photograph shows one of many Civil War cemeteries that serve as the final resting place for the more than 200,000 Union and Confederate soldiers who lost their lives on the battlefields. Four hundred thousand additional soldiers died from diseases contracted during the war.

An illustration showing a runaway slave pursued by slave hunters and their dog. The Fugitive Slave Act of 1850 spawned a bounty hunter "industry." Bounty hunters could earn handsome rewards for capturing and returning runaway slaves. Douglass and other abolitionists spoke out angrily against the law.

people were still permitted to own slaves), but slavery was allowed for the territories of Texas, New Mexico, and Utah. Both sides were unhappy, and Frederick condemned the Compromise.

As an appeasement to pro-slavery forces, the Compromise included the Fugitive Slave Act of 1850, which strengthened the Fugitive Slave Act that had originally been enacted in 1793. The newer version of the act made capturing escaped slaves a federal responsibility, whereas previously it had been up to the states. Now, states were required to cooperate with federal marshals and other authorities in tracking and capturing escaped slaves. The act pleased lawmakers from the South. They had been unhappy with what they perceived as a lack of will in enforcing federal slave laws. In the North, the act was received far less favorably, and with Douglass leading the way, abolitionists expressed pure, undiluted outrage.

By 1854, angry abolitionists were attacking jails and courthouses to free captured runaway slaves. In Boston, the site of the famous Boston Tea

Party, 50,000 citizens turned out to protest a slave, in handcuffs, being led to a ship and returned to Virginia. That same year, Wisconsin declared the Fugitive Slave Act unconstitutional. The Republican Party, dedicated to ending slavery, was formed there. Douglass would later join the party. He remained a loyal Republican for the rest of his life.

Bleeding Kansas

Kansas Territory had its own version of civil war ahead of the rest of the nation, when in 1854 the question arose as to whether it would enter the Union as a slave or free state. At one point, two governments were formed for the territory (only one of them recognized at any one time by the U.S. government), one pro-slavery, the other abolitionist. During a period known as "Bleeding Kansas," each side formed a volunteer militia, and violence broke out. A man named John Brown led a small band of armed abolitionists into battle, killed some pro-slavery militiamen, and captured others. President James Buchanan declared Brown an outlaw and put a price on his head of $250 (about $5,000 in today's economy). Brown scoffed at this and put a price of two dollars and 50 cents ($50) on Buchanan's head.

A portrait of militant abolitionist John Brown (1800-1859). After Brown led armed attacks against pro-slavery forces in Kansas in 1854, he became a fugitive and grew a beard to help hide his identity. He consulted with Frederick Douglass before his infamous attack five years later at Harpers Ferry, Virginia.

The fight over slavery was further fueled by a legal case that went all the way to the U.S. Supreme Court. Dred Scott was a slave who had lived with his master, an army surgeon, in the free state of Illinois and the free territory of Wisconsin. When Scott's master died, Scott filed a lawsuit to win his freedom in the courts. In a decision known as "Dred Scott v. Sanford," the Court ruled seven to two that Scott had to be returned to his current owner.

This ruling worked in the interest of slave states and slaveholders. It was a major blow to abolitionist forces and dashed the hopes of slaves who sought freedom and protection by the federal government.

A Man of Many Causes

All this time, as he remained fierce in his determination to bring slavery to an end, Frederick also started with equal passion to address other issues. Education was one. Even in the liberal city of Rochester, schools were segregated. In New York, one of every 40 students was African American, but only one dollar of every $1,600 marked for education went to black schools. One hundred years before the Supreme Court would finally rule that state laws protecting school segregation were illegal (Brown v. Board of Education, 1954), Frederick used his newspaper to campaign for desegregation. In 1857, Rochester schools were integrated. Equal education was a fight that Frederick would continue after the Civil War and the abolition of slavery.

This 1957 photograph shows soldiers escorting black students into Little Rock Central High School in Arkansas. Despite a U.S. Supreme Court ruling that schools must be integrated, Arkansas governor Orville Faubus refused to comply until President Dwight Eisenhower ordered in the federal troops to enforce the law. To Frederick Douglass and other abolitionists of the 1800s, equal education was almost as important as the right to vote.

> *People might not get all they work for in this world, but they must certainly work for all they get.*
>
> — Frederick Douglass, "Self-Made Men"

"Self-Made Men"

Another one of Douglass' concerns was not really political at all. It had to do with character and personal achievement. In 1859, on the brink of the Civil War, Douglass delivered a lecture called "Self-Made Men." It turned out to be the most popular speech he ever gave. He delivered this lecture more than 50 times between 1859 and 1893.

The theme of this speech is that anyone can achieve success through hard work and determination. A person born poor or black had to work harder, but success was still possible. This view, that hard work and perseverance can lead to personal success, is often called "The American Dream." In "Self-Made Men," Douglass explains the forces behind the turning points in his life. Luck had something to do with it. God had something to do with it. More than anything else, it was his own hard work and determination that made possible the successes in his life.

A "What-if?" of History

The riskiest thing Frederick Douglass did since his escape occurred in 1858, was to invite John Brown over to his house. It was not a social call. Brown, the same John Brown who led the anti-slavery raids in "Bleeding Kansas," was hatching a plan. The plan was to lead an armed slave revolt in Harpers Ferry, Virginia. He asked Frederick to help him work out the details. Frederick agreed. He also asked Frederick to join him on the raid. Here Frederick drew the line. In 1859, Brown carried out his plan. It was bloody, and it failed. Brown and the surviving members of his troop were arrested, tried, and hanged. Had Douglass decided to join Brown, he surely would have been killed in battle or executed. This remains one of the great "what-ifs" of American history.

JOHN BROWN — THE MARTYR.

Meeting a Slave Mother and her Child on the steps of Charlestown Jail on his way to Execution. Regarding them with a look of compassion Captain Brown stooped and kissed the Child then his fate.

An 1859 illustration shows a brave and defiant John Brown being led from jail to the gallows for his execution. By 1859, many abolitionists had let go of their strict, pacifist doctrines, and John Brown became a heroic symbol to many in the fight against slavery.

Still, Frederick was a co-conspirator. With a warrant issued for his arrest, he fled to Canada. From there he sailed to England, where he lectured for six months. The death of his daughter, Annie, brought him back. There were no federal agents waiting to arrest him. It was 1860. With the issue of slavery threatening to tear the nation in two, the Justice Department lost interest in enforcing the warrant.

Taking Issue with the President

In the presidential election of 1860, the Democrats were mostly pro-slavery and the Republicans were mostly anti-slavery. Douglass supported the Republican candidate, Abraham Lincoln, believing that Lincoln could win and that he represented the best hope to end slavery in the United States.

Lincoln did win. Within six months of his election, 11 southern states seceded from the United States and formed their own country, the Confederate States of America. On April 12, 1861, Confederate forces attacked a Union military facility at Fort Sumter, South Carolina, and the Civil War had begun.

Douglass voted for Lincoln, but he had some issues to take up with the new president. First of all, Douglass wanted Lincoln to call for an immediate end to all slavery. Lincoln wanted to bring all the states back

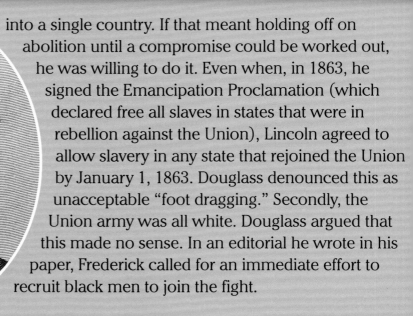

LINCOLN

into a single country. If that meant holding off on abolition until a compromise could be worked out, he was willing to do it. Even when, in 1863, he signed the Emancipation Proclamation (which declared free all slaves in states that were in rebellion against the Union), Lincoln agreed to allow slavery in any state that rejoined the Union by January 1, 1863. Douglass denounced this as unacceptable "foot dragging." Secondly, the Union army was all white. Douglass argued that this made no sense. In an editorial he wrote in his paper, Frederick called for an immediate effort to recruit black men to join the fight.

Uncle Sam Wants You

Douglass' lobbying on his second grievance with the president paid off in 1863, when Congress passed a law allowing black men to serve in the Union army. Frederick immediately went to work recruiting for the 54th Massachusetts Regiment. Frederick's sons, Charles and Lewis, were among the first to enlist. Frederick Douglass, Jr., also worked as a recruiter. Before it was over, 180,000 African-American soldiers served in the Civil War on the Union side.

Soon after the election of Abraham Lincoln (top) as president, 11 states seceded from the United States to form their own country, the Confederate States of America. They formed their own army, elected their own president (Jefferson Davis), issued their own currency, and fought under their own battle and naval flags (middle). The map at the bottom shows the boundaries between the free and slave states and territories, most of which would become the basis for the alignment of states in the Civil War.

Right: a detail from the 1897 Memorial to Robert Gould Shaw designed by Augustus Saint-Gaudens and Stanford White. Shaw served as colonel for the all-black 54th Massachusetts Volunteer Infantry. When the Civil War began, African Americans were not allowed to serve as soldiers in the Union army. Frederick Douglass campaigned successfully to change this regulation. Lower right: an original recruitment poster for the 54th. The "bounty" was a sign-up bonus.

TO COLORED MEN.
54th REGIMENT!
MASSACHUSETTS VOLUNTEERS,
OF
AFRICAN DESCENT!
$100 BOUNTY!
At the expiration of the term of service.
PAY, $13 A MONTH!
AND
STATE AID TO FAMILIES.
RECRUITING OFFICE,
Cor. Cambridge & North Russell Sts., Boston.
Lieut. J. W. M. APPLETON, Recruiting Officer.
J. E. FARWELL & Co., Steam Job Printers. No. 37 Congress Street, Boston.

The Confederacy declared that any black soldiers captured would be treated as runaway slaves subject to execution. Lincoln was swift to respond. For every prisoner of war executed by the Confederates, the Union would kill a rebel soldier. Douglass applauded Lincoln's declaration.

Welcome to the White House

Frederick's respect for the president continued to grow when Lincoln invited him to a White House meeting. Although African-American regiments were fighting battles and sacrificing lives for the Union cause, black soldiers did not receive pay equal to white soldiers. Frederick made his case to the president for an end to this discrimination. Frederick won some concessions, but they were small. Frederick argued for this cause with Lincoln and his successors for years, even after the end of the war.

Frederick and President Lincoln soon became close. As an adviser to the president, Frederick urged Lincoln to lay the groundwork for constitutional amendments that would give voting and civil rights to black men. At a second meeting in the White House, Lincoln shared with Frederick his dark and private fear that the Union might lose the war.

In case that happened, he asked Frederick to prepare a plan to help slaves escape to the North. It was a frightening possibility.

A Sad Loss

On April 9, 1865—almost exactly four years after it started—the Civil War came to an end when Confederate general Robert E. Lee signed an unconditional surrender to Union general Ulysses S. Grant. Tragically, 200,000 soldiers died in battle over the course of the conflict, and many more from disease. Then, less than a week after the surrender, President Lincoln was shot dead as he and his wife watched a play in Washington, D.C.

Memorial services were held around the country. Frederick lost a leader and a dear friend. He gave moving eulogies in Rochester and Boston. Mrs. Lincoln sent Frederick her husband's cane as a keepsake. At the funeral procession in New York City, however, Douglass and other African Americans were not allowed to participate. There was obviously still much work to be done.

This photograph from 1865 shows the New York funeral procession for Abraham Lincoln. Lincoln had been assassinated just a few days before. Although they initially disagreed about issues such as the timing of the abolition of slavery, Douglass and Lincoln became close political allies and friends.

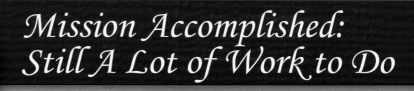

CHAPTER SIX

Mission Accomplished: Still A Lot of Work to Do

In 1860, there were 4,000,000 slaves in the United States. At the end of 1865, there were none. With the ratification of the 13th (1865), 14th (1868), and 15th (1870) amendments to the U.S. Constitution, slavery was formally abolished, the Bill of Rights was guaranteed to all people regardless of race, and the right to vote was extended to all men regardless of race. The goals of the abolitionists had been achieved. Frederick's former mentor, William Lloyd Garrison, was ready to disband the American Anti-Slavery Society. Many abolitionists left the movement. Even Frederick thought about buying a farm and retiring.

A newspaper illustration used to help announce Frederick Douglass' speaking engagement at a local church. After the Civil War, Douglass became something of an honored celebrity, and his appearances were treated as news.

Slavery Reinvented

Slavery was abolished, but the South did not blossom into a garden of equality. The same people who were pro-slavery before the Civil War clung to racial prejudices and hatred. New laws were passed in southern states that were designed to hold back African Americans and deny them the

In 1865, a secret organization of terrorist vigilantes, the Ku Klux Klan, was formed in the South. The Klan and other groups used violence and intimidation to keep African Americans from voting, learning to read, and exercising other rights they had gained following the Civil War. In the first of these two illustrations from *Harper's Weekly* magazine, a group of Klan members is shown in 1871 (left) at the time of their arrest for the attempted murder of an African-American family. The second illustration (below) is an artist's rendition of the attempted murder. It shows the Klansmen at the door, one with a rifle, as the family gathers to prepare its evening meal.

full rights and opportunities due them. Freedmen without jobs could be fined and forced to work in slave-like conditions. In some states, they could not buy land. The more federal laws guaranteed the rights of all Americans, the more southern states connived ways around those laws and practiced new, harsh forms of discrimination. The new chains were racial bigotry. The new whips were intimidation and violence.

No Thank You, Mr. President

Putting aside any thoughts of retirement, Douglass lectured throughout the North. He warned that the evils of racial prejudice and discrimination had taken on new forms in the South and that old slaveholders were actually gaining the upper hand. In February of 1866, Frederick met with Lincoln's successor, President Andrew Johnson. Frederick was hopeful that with Johnson's help they would reverse this dangerous trend, but Johnson was not sympathetic. He showed little interest in protecting the voting rights and freedoms of African Americans. The next year, Johnson offered Frederick the post of commissioner of the Freedmen's Bureau. Until southern states pressured Congress to abolish it, the Bureau was in charge of building hospitals and schools to improve conditions for freedmen. Frederick suspected that Johnson only wanted to use his name for his own political gain. He turned down the President's offer.

Douglass was disappointed with Johnson, but he stuck with the Republican Party. In 1868 and again in 1872, he campaigned for the successful elections of Ulysses S. Grant. Frederick hoped to receive a political appointment from Grant, but despite his firm support, Grant passed him by. To earn money and keep up his fight for civil rights, Frederick stepped up his lecturing and public appearances.

More Turning Points

Just as the oppression of African Americans in the South had reinvented itself in the form of restrictive laws and harsh forms of bigotry and intimidation, Frederick Douglass was not done reinventing himself, either. As a man of principal and independent thinking, he even risked his reputation as a supporter of universal rights for all Americans, including women. In 1869, he broke with his friends Susan B. Anthony and Elizabeth Cady Stanton on a single issue—women's voting rights. Anthony and Stanton opposed the 15th Amendment unless it gave the right to vote to women as well as to black men. Frederick insisted that in this case a woman's right to vote could wait.

In 1870, Douglass resumed his career as a publisher. He ran and owned a weekly newspaper, the *New National Era*. With the help of his sons, Frederick used this paper as a platform to cheer civil rights victories and to lobby for additional gains. Unfortunately, the paper had a low circulation, and it went bankrupt in 1874. Frederick lost much of his personal investment.

In 1872, a "protest" political party was formed. It was called the Equal Rights Party. Their convention nominated a woman, Victoria Woodhull, as its presidential candidate. The convention also nominated, without his consent, Frederick Douglass as Woodhull's vice presidential running mate. Technically, he was the first African American to run for vice president of the United States. In reality, Frederick was a Republican, and he never gave his support to the Equal Rights Party. Instead, Frederick campaigned for the reelection of President Ulysses S. Grant.

The 1870s also brought misfortune that affected the Douglass family's pocketbook. In 1872, Frederick's house in Rochester burned down. Arson was suspected. No one was hurt, but Frederick used this setback as a reason to move his family to Washington, D.C. There, in 1874, Frederick was appointed president of the Freedmen's Savings and Trust Company. The FSTC was founded to help African Americans save money and invest. When Frederick took charge, the bank was in deep trouble and on the verge of collapse. Frederick went to Congress for a kind of "bailout," and he invested his own money.

Frederick was willing to take the same risk as everyone else who had a bank account there. Unfortunately, the FSTC failed anyway. Many lost their savings. The Douglasses lost $12,000 of their own money, an amount worth about $180,000 today.

Undated photo portrait of Victoria Woodhull. Woodhull was one of the most controversial figures of the 1800s, partly because she advocated "free love" and workers' rights against the wealthy class. Woodhull was also the first female stock broker and presidential candidate.

Back on the Lecture Circuit

Frederick went back on the lecture circuit to supplement his income. As he traveled, Douglass protested discrimination and segregation wherever he found it, or wherever it found him. If he was not treated fairly in a hotel or restaurant, he would publish a letter in the local paper. He understood the power of the press and knew how to use negative publicity to put pressure on businesses.

Political Appointments

In election after election, Frederick continued to campaign hard for the Republican candidates. In appreciation for his support, President Rutherford B. Hayes chose Frederick as the U.S. Marshal of the District of Columbia. This appointment put Douglass in charge of the criminal justice system in and around Washington, D.C. This was a groundbreaking appointment for an African American, and it would lead to more.

With the money he earned from his lectures and political appointments, Frederick purchased a beautiful estate in the Washington area. It had 20 rooms. It was on an estate that originally consisted of nine acres (3.6 hectares) and then grew to 15 acres (six ha) when Douglass bought more land the following year. It housed oil paintings and a library. At the age of 60, Frederick Douglass had risen from a child slave in tattered clothes to a man of distinction and wealth.

The Life and Times

In 1881, when Frederick was 63, another Republican president, James A. Garfield, awarded him the job of Recorder of Deeds for the District of Columbia. His office kept track of all property sales in the area. As with similar political appointments, the pay was very good, and it was less than full-time work. That year, he tackled the third installment of his autobiography. *Life and Times of Frederick Douglass* greatly expanded the details of his life as a slave and brought his life as a freedman up to date. Frederick would revise *Life and Times* in 1892, and that edition has become the "definitive" story of his life.

This 1877 illustration from a Washington, D.C., newspaper shows African-American citizens lined up to congratulate Frederick Douglass upon his appointment as marshal, while a white staffer sits unenthusiastically in the corner. Some white people, especially in the South, did not appreciate Douglass' breakthrough political achievements.

This modern photograph shows the Douglass' Washington, D.C., home, Cedar Hill. Douglass' income from lectures and his political appointments allowed him to live his life in comfort. Today, you can tour Cedar Hill and see many of the original furnishings and household belongings.

Personal sadness struck Frederick in 1882. After an illness that left her paralyzed, his wife Anna died. It was Anna who had helped Frederick escape from Baltimore, and Anna who managed the Rochester home. For many dozens of runaway slaves, she made the house a comfortable and safe "station" on the Underground Railroad. She and Frederick were married for 44 years.

The Controversial Ambassador

Two years later, Frederick Douglass married Helen Pitts. Helen was an educated woman from a family that had supported women's rights, abolition, and social progress. Frederick was 66. Helen was 46. Frederick, of course, was black. Helen was white. Theirs was the most high-profile interracial marriage of the era. Washington society was shocked. Helen's family stopped speaking to her. Frederick's children were angry.

Frederick and Helen ignored all the criticism. Frederick wrote, "My first wife was the color of my mother, my second is the color of my father." After Frederick's death, it was Helen who organized his papers and started what would become the Frederick Douglass Memorial and Historical Association.

After a long tour of Europe in 1886–1887, Helen and Frederick returned to the Washington home. By now, Frederick Douglass was honored and respected by most of America. It was common to see photographs of him with presidents and dignitaries. He was nicknamed "The Lion of Anacostia," after the Anacostia neighborhood where he lived.

Frederick continued to serve his country. He worked as a diplomat in both Haiti and the Dominican Republic. He also continued to speak up for social justice. On February 20, 1895, he attended a women's rights meeting. That night, he suffered a heart attack and died at the age of 77.

The Legacy of the Lion

Frederick Douglass is widely recognized for his role in the abolition of slavery and for helping win the fight for Constitutional rights for all Americans regardless of race. He achieved excellence in speaking and writing. He was a pioneer in the history of African American literature, newspapers and publishing, school desegregation, and government leadership.

A photograph of the simple graves of Frederick (right) and Helen (left) Douglass. The inscription on Helen's stone reads: "Through her vision his greatness was memorialized at Cedar Hill in Washington, D.C." The inscription also says that "Mrs. Douglass was the founder of the Frederick Douglass Memorial and Historical Association."

September 3, the day Frederick Bailey escaped from slavery, is celebrated as Frederick Douglass Freedom Day. This day is marked by programs and essay contests at many schools throughout the United States. It was begun by Frederick Douglass' great-great grandson (Frederick IV) and his wife, B.J. As part of the observances, Frederick IV and B.J. portray Frederick and Anna Douglass, visit students, and put on educational shows. They dress in clothing that free blacks of the middle class in the 1800s might have worn. In doing so, they emphasize that not all African Americans in the 1800s were slaves and that even those who were born into slavery aspired to become members of a free society.

This Frederick Douglass mural on the Freedom Wall in Belfast, Northern Ireland, stands as an international tribute to Frederick Douglass. Douglass made two trips to Ireland and Great Britain—one during his exile for 21 months in 1845–1846 after he published his *Narrative*, the second in 1859 when the authorities were chasing him for his connections to John Brown.

Inspired by two Irishmen to escape from slavery Frederick Douglass came to Ireland during the famine. Henceforth he championed the abolition of slavery, women's rights and Irish freedom.

FREDERICK DOUGLASS (1818-1895)

'Perhaps no class has carried prejudice against colour to a point more dangerous than have the Irish and yet no people have been more relentlessly oppressed on account of race and religion.' -Frederick Douglass

A Hero Today

More than 100 years after his death, Frederick Douglass is very much with us as a hero of the anti-slavery cause. His life also stands as inspirational proof that with the right amounts of will, courage, determination, and support from one's fellow human beings, we are capable of rising above even the harshest, most cruel conditions of our birth.

The illustration above, from the 1881 illustrated edition of *The Life and Times of Frederick Douglass*, shows the young slave, Frederick Bailey, first learning to read. The 1880 photograph shown right shows Frederick Douglass, the public official who would soon go on to become his country's diplomat and statesman. His achievements in between—abolitionist, speaker, writer, publisher, businessman, and advisor to presidents—make his life remarkable, not just as an African American, but as an American.

Chronology

1818 (Exact date unknown) Frederick Douglass is born as Frederick Augustus Washington Bailey, a slave in Maryland.

1826–1833 Frederick lives in Baltimore as a slave servant to Hugh and Sophia Auld.

1833 Frederick makes the first of three attempts to escape. It fails.

1834 Frederick is hired out to Edward Covey, a "slave breaker," to break his spirit and make him accept slavery.

1836 Frederick's plan to attempt his second escape from slavery is discovered.

1836–38 Frederick works in the Baltimore shipyards as a caulker. He falls in love with Anna Murray, a free black woman.

1838 He escapes from slavery, goes to New York City, marries Anna Murray, and settles in New Bedford, Massachusetts. He renames himself Frederick Douglass.

1841 Frederick speaks at an anti-slavery meeting for the first time. He becomes a professional speaker for William Lloyd Garrison's American Anti-Slavery Society.

1845 Frederick publishes his autobiographical *Narrative of the Life of Frederick Douglass, An American Slave, Written by Himself*. He tours Ireland and Britain as an anti-slavery speaker.

1846 Supporters in Britain purchase his freedom.

1847 He returns to the United States a free man and moves to Rochester, New York, to publish a weekly newspaper, the *North Star*.

1848 He attends the first Women's Rights Convention in Seneca Falls, New York, and signs The Declaration of Sentiments.

1851 He helps three fugitive Maryland slaves escape to Canada as a "Station Master" at the Rochester Underground Railroad.

1852 He splits with Garrison over the means to achieve the abolition of slavery.

1855 Frederick publishes his second autobiography, *My Bondage and My Freedom*.

1857 Through Douglass' efforts, Rochester public schools are desegregated.

1859–1860 Frederick helps John Brown plan a slave revolt. Frederick escapes to Canada and then to Great Britain to avoid being arrested for helping plan the revolt. He returns upon hearing of his daughter's death.

1861 The Civil War begins. Douglass lobbies for the use of African-American troops to fight the Confederacy.

1863 The Emancipation Proclamation abolishes slavery in the states that are in rebellion against the Union. Douglass recruits for the 54th Massachusetts Infantry, the first regiment of African-American soldiers. He meets with President Lincoln to discuss the unequal pay and poor treatment black soldiers receive.

1863–1864 Douglass serves as Lincoln's adviser.

1864 Frederick meets with Lincoln again. In case the war is not a total Union victory, Lincoln asks Douglass to prepare an effort to help slaves escape to the North.

1865 April 14, Lincoln is assassinated. The Thirteenth Amendment to the Constitution, outlawing slavery, is ratified by Congress.

1866 Douglass attends the convention of Women's Equal Rights Association and clashes with women's rights leaders over their insistence that the vote not be extended to black men unless it is given to all women at the same time.

1872 Frederick's Rochester home is mysteriously destroyed by fire. He moves his family to Washington, D.C. He is nominated for vice president by the Equal Rights Party on a ticket headed by Victoria Woodhull but maintains his support for candidates from the Republican Party.

1874 He is named president of the troubled Freedmen's Savings and Trust Company. The bank ultimately fails.

1877 He is appointed U.S. Marshal for the District of Columbia.

1878 Frederick purchases Cedar Hill, a 9-acre (3.6 hectares) estate in the Anacostia section of Washington, D.C. The following year, he purchases more land to bring the total area up to about 15 acres (six ha).

1881 Douglass is appointed Recorder of Deeds for the District of Columbia. He publishes his third autobiography, *Life and Times of Frederick Douglass*.

1882 Anna Murray Douglass dies.

1884 Frederick marries his secretary, Helen Pitts.

1889–1891 Frederick serves as minister and consul to Haiti.

1892–1893 Frederick receives joint U.S. diplomatic appointments in the Dominican Republic and Haiti.

1895 Frederick Douglass dies at his home of a heart attack.

1898 A statue of Frederick Douglass, the first monument to a black man in the United States, is unveiled in Rochester.

abolitionist A person dedicated to ending, or abolishing, the practice of slavery. Abolitionist leaders included William Lloyd Garrison, Harriet Tubman, James Birney, and Frederick Douglass.

appendix Printed information at the end of a book. After the story of the main subject is done, the appendix can offer additional background information.

bailout A form of assistance given to a business or some other organization to help prevent it from collapsing financially

boycott An organized protest, usually in the form of a refusal to use or buy someone else's products or services

caulker Someone who fills in cracks with a waterproof substance called a sealant.

charisma Personal appeal, charm, or energy that attracts others

diplomat A person who serves as his or her country's official representative to another country

docile Willing to be supervised or bossed around. Slave masters wanted their slaves to be docile.

federal Having to do with a central government, such as a national government, as opposed to the governments of the units (states) that make up a nation

foreshadow To give a warning or indication of a future event

hypocrisy The practice of saying one thing but practicing another. Frederick Douglass exposed the hypocrisy of many northerners who said they believed in racial equality but practiced racial discrimination.

idealistic Basing policies or actions on one's political or moral beliefs or on what one considers to be a perfect situation

incumbent The current holder of a position, usually used to describe someone who is running for reelection to a political office

investment Putting money into a business with the expectation of receiving some kind of reward or return

irony The use of words to say something that is the opposite of what they seem to mean

lawsuit A claim or a dispute that is brought to a court of law to be settled

memoir A written account of the author's personal experiences. Frederick Douglass' three autobiographical books are memoirs.

metaphor Language in which often vivid words or terms are used for effect to describe something completely different. A term often used to describe Douglass—"The Lion of Anacostia"—was a metaphor suggesting that he was a strong and proud fighter for political change. Douglass' speeches and writings often contained skillful use of metaphor.

middle class A segment of society that falls between the wealthy upper class and the working class. Usually made up of professional and business workers, the middle class is usually thought to represent the mainstream of U.S. society in terms of income, lifestyle, and values.

militia A military force raised from the local populace, usually to support or supplement the regular military

naive Showing innocence or a lack of experience or good judgment

novella A work of fiction that is longer than a short story but shorter than a novel

orator A skilled public speaker. Both William Lloyd Garrison and Frederick Douglass were effective orators.

overseer A person who is in charge of other people or an organization. In times of slavery, the overseer worked for the slave owner and managed the work of the slaves.

skeptical Doubting the truth of something

vehement Showing strong, intense, or emotional feelings

vigilantes People who take matters of law enforcement into their own hands, often with the belief that officials do not do a satisfactory job of enforcing laws

Further Information

Books

Altman, Linda Jacobs. *Slavery and Abolition in America.* Enslow Publishers, 1999.

Deford, Deborah C. *African Americans During the Civil War.* (Slavery in America). Chelsea House Publications, 2006.

Douglass, Frederick. *Narrative of the Life of Frederick Douglass, an American Slave, Written by Himself.* Simon & Schuster, 2004.

Miller, Douglass. *Frederick Douglass and the Fight for Freedom.* Replica Books, 2002.

Osborne, Linda Barrett. *Traveling the Freedom Road: From Slavery and the Civil War Through Reconstruction.* Abrams Books for Young Readers, 2009.

Zeimert, Karen. *The* Amistad *Slave Revolt and American Abolition.* Linnet Books, 1997.

Videos

Frederick Douglass. A 50-minute video of Frederick Douglass' life from A&E Studio's Biography Series.

Web Sites

www.frederickdouglassrc.com/default.asp
Official site of the Frederick Douglass Resource Center in Rochester, New York. The site offers a video of his life and information about current events that celebrate his life and work.

www.frederickdouglassiv.org/
Official site of the Frederick Douglass Organization, featuring archives and photos of Frederick Douglass as well as an extensive time line of important events in his life.

www.nps.gov/history/museum/exhibits/douglass/index.html
The National Park System's official Frederick Douglass Historic Site Web page. It features samples of his writings, a virtual tour of Cedar Hill, and many images and photographs.

www.yale.edu/glc/events/dpnotice.htm
The site of the Yale University Frederick Douglass Book Prize. It lists the annual winners with a description of each book.

Index

About the Author

Henry Elliot lives in Pittsburgh. He is active in neighborhood restoration projects, and he spends much time walking along the banks of Pittsburgh's three rivers, the Allegheny, the Monongahela, and the Ohio.

Printed in the USA—BG